Bosh and Flapdoodle

Also by A. R. Ammons

Ommateum
Expressions of Sea Level
Corsons Inlet
Tape for the Turn of the Year
Northfield Poems
Selected Poems
Uplands
Briefings
Collected Poems: 1951–1971
(winner of the National Book Award for Poetry, 1973)
Sphere: The Form of Motion
(winner of the 1973–1974 Bollingen Prize in Poetry)
Diversifications
The Snow Poems
Highgate Roate
The Selected Poems: 1951–1977
Selected Longer Poems
A Coast of Trees
(winner of the National Book Critics Circle Award for Poetry, 1981)
Worldly Hopes
Lake Effect Country
The Selected Poems: Expanded Edition
Sumerian Vistas
The Really Short Poems
Garbage
(winner of the National Book Award for Poetry, 1993)
Brink Road
Glare

A. R. Ammons

Bosh and Flapdoodle

W. W. Norton & Company

New York London

Selected poems have appeared in *American Poetry Review, Hudson Review, Kenyon Review, Michigan Quarterly Review, Poetry East, Slate,* and *Epoch.*

For information about permission to reproduce selections from this book,
write to Permissions, W. W. Norton & Company, Inc.,
500 Fifth Avenue, New York, NY 10110

Manufacturing by The Courier Companies, Inc.
Book design by Blue Shoe Studio
Production manager: Andrew Marasia

Library of Congress Cataloging-in-Publication Data
Ammons, A. R., 1926–
Bosh and flapdoodle : poems / A.R. Ammons.— 1st ed.
p. cm.
ISBN 0-393-05952-9 (hardcover)
I. Title.
PS3501.M6B67 2005
811'.54—dc22

2004026050

ISBN 978-0-393-32895-0

W. W. Norton & Company, Inc., 500 Fifth Avenue, New York, N.Y. 10110
www.wwnorton.com

W. W. Norton & Company Ltd., Castle House,
75/76 Wells Street, London W1T 3QT

2 3 4 5 6 7 8 9 0

Contents

A Note of Appreciation

These poems were written in 1996, though my father continued to work on the collection until shortly before he died. No poems have been added or deleted. The order of the poems as well as the title of the book are his. The poems have been left exactly as Ammons wrote them. We have not attempted to change the spelling or sense of his words to conform with standard spelling or usage.

My mother and I are deeply grateful to friends and colleagues of my late father who encouraged us to publish the collection, among them, Mike Abrams, Roald Hoffmann, David Lehman, Ken McClane, Steve Tapscott, our agent Glen Hartley, Norton editor Jill Bialosky and her assistant, Sarah Moriarty, and Emily Wilson for her lively enthusiasm for Ammons's poetry.

We are especially indebted to Roger Gilbert for his steadfast dedication and help with all aspects of the project, and to Helen Vendler, who so generously read the manuscript, for her guidance and warm response.

—John Ammons
Mill Valley, California

Bosh and Flapdoodle

Fasting

Not two months off till the shortest day, the
shadows near noon all flop over one way as if

it were soon to be dusk: that's winter coming
all right, slanted over, long-casting, &

pale: the trees are suddenly bristled
stripped: did the sun steam a frost up and melt

the leaves: probably not: squirrels shook
the leaves out of the lofts: some (people)

are strict, spare, and pure; some strew gems
in the mud: I perforce raise the level of the

mud till it endows shining, like lake
ice or sunny water or like a distant field of

pumpkins, leafless and unpicked, or even like
the first rye fields against gray woods, so

bright green: hark, the jewels are lost in
the general rising, and the rare and priceless

are cheapened by white towers in a still-blue
day: of course, you can't wear an image, a

windchurned figure from a volcano core, on
your finger, and some thoughts are too grand

to diadem a brain: (the tree by the road now
looks like a sketch for a tree): Halloween

needs what we have today—a stir: not a gale
so constant and high but gusts that show up

out of nowhere, presences that are not there,
little twirls of leaves that scoot across the

street and then just wilt out, forms,
air-whorls that are made out of nothing

but that touch your face or rustle into the
bushes, whispering and hissing: all kinds of

cases where motion charges the show
and where motion gives its form away by

picking up miscellany and throwing it off, motion
the closest cousin to spirit and spirit the

closest neighbor to the other world, haunted
with possibility, hope, anguish, and alarm.

Reverse Reserve and You Have Reverse

This morning, with small swirls of the season's
first snowflakes dropping and rising in the

air, a bushy black dog, his head high, his
tongue aloll, his tail also high, comes down

the street: lost, he looks wildly all around,
turns into and out of driveways, reverses

his run and goes back to places as unfamiliar
as if he had never come through them: my wife

has lost her taste for eggs: she would rather
have a piece of toast with raspberry jam and

a little (real) butter than over, scrambled,
poached or boiled hard: I ask her, where has

the taste gone, but it's just like losing yr
dog, she doesn't know where it is: eggs in

popovers are still found in her taste: she
just loves popovers, with jam, I mean, and

a little (real) butter: cultural conditioning
has changed us so we have to look at the apes,

the gorillas, chimps, and babs to see what a
little cultural conditioning does: if we

didn't have cultural conditioning, we males
would (as we sometimes still do) soften up the

females with attention or pursuit to bend them to
the primary imperative: for baboons, you

know, females, wouldn't want an infant swinging
from their belly or arms or riding on their

backs if it wasn't for estrus compelling them:
we already know that women prefer romance and

cuddling to anything invasive: whereas, we
males desire above all to get it in and get

rid of it: sometimes women will snarl, fake
headaches, pretend to be asleep because who

wants to risk her life having babies and lose
her life taking care of them, you might say:

so males have to hold them up a little into
mindless obedience so the sperm can run: of

course, we are so cultivated now that the
woman can stand right in the kitchen and

refuse to get on the table: where does that
leave the urgent one with his outstanding

example of firmness in hand: it is, then,
without doubt the sharpness of male need that

perpetuates the species (which, truly, might
better be left alone):

RULLY OUSTSTANDING

Surface Effects

Nature, you know, is not a one-way street: its
most consistent figure is turning—turning

back, turning in, turning around: why?, because
it has nowhere to go but into itself: all its

motions are intermediate: if carrion turns
into flight (as it becomes in the wings of

buzzards) why it is not long before flight is
carrion again: of course, if nature *is* a

one-way street it is some kind of superlative
avenue, some large summary that takes its

account from time—that is, if time is a
one-way street: that is, if time, too, doesn't

bend back into itself and start its intermediaries
over again: if, for example, dry years cause

the brook to cut its way one-sided, maybe that
deepens at least that narrow flow so fish can

get up the ledges to the pools and sleepy
shallows: or the worn-out ledge grist may

make a place downstream to put a willow in: so
nature, turning, does not turn on itself, for

whatever it turns into is nature anew: Mars,
desolate on the surface, doesn't mind desolation:

Venus's boiling stones are just a lit merriment:
the hillside, drenched by rain after wild

fires, doesn't mind collapsing: what is wrong
for us is wrong for us; we may even

be wrong in reckoning it wrong; it may be
right, and we haven't yet learned how: when

we correct wrongs, we may interfere with
the swing-around that will bring things right,

possibly righter than they were before:
don't worry about nature: it is always nature:

when we divert water into California's valley
deserts, we produce mucho melons, but we

leave the salty mouth of the Colorado dry: we
play our arrogances small scale: slowly we

learn that surplus carbon monoxide feeds a soil
microorganism: the large designs are filigrees

through which nearly still measures move, turn, split,
come and go again.

Aubade

They say, lose weight, change your lifestyle:
that's, take the life out of your style and

the style out of your life: give up fats,
give up sweets, chew rabbit greens, raw: and

how about carrots: raw: also, wear your
hipbones out walking: we were designed for

times when breakfast was not always there, and
you had to walk a mile, maybe, for your first

berry or you had to chip off a flint before
you could dig up a root: and there were

times when like going off to a weight reduction
center you had a belly full of nothing: easy

to be skinny digesting bark: but here now at
the breakfast buffet or lavish brunch you're

trapped between resistance and getting your
money's worth and the net gain from that

transaction is about one pound more: hunting
and gathering is a better lifestyle than

resisting: resisting works up your nerves
not your appetite (already substantial in the

wild) and burns up fewer calories than the
activity arising from hunger pangs: all in

all this is a praise for modern life—who
wants to pick the subrealities from his teeth

every minute—but all this is just not what
we were designed for, bad as it was: any way

I go now I feel I'm going against nature, when
I feel so free with the ways and means, the

dynamics, the essentialities honed out clearly
from millions of years: sometimes when I say

"you" in my poems and appear to be addressing
the lord above, I'm personifying the contours

of the onhigh, the ways by which the world
works, however hard to see: for the onhigh

is every time the on low, too, and in the
middle: one lifts up one's voice to the

lineations of singing and sings, in effect,
you, you are the one, the center, it is around

you that the comings and goings gather, you
are the before and after, the around and

through: in all your motions you are ever
still, constant as motion itself: there with

you we abide, abide the changes, abide the
dissolutions and recommencements of our very

selves, abide in your abiding: but, of course
I don't mean "you" as anyone in particular

but I mean the center of motions millions of
years have taught us to seek: now, with

space travel and gene therapy that "you" has
moved out of the woods and rocks and streams

and traveled on out so far in space that it
rounds the whole and is, in a way, nowhere to

be found or congratulated, and so what is out
there dwells in our heads now as a bit of

yearning, maybe vestigial, and it is a yearning
like a painful sweetness, a nearly reachable

presence that nearly feels like love, something
we can put aside as we get up to rustle up a

little breakfast or contemplate a little
weight loss, or gladden the morning by getting

off to work. . . .

Oil Ode

My wife says that the two guys on TV say that
the most important thing is changing the oil:

and my wife says this friend of hers said go
over to Doug's Fish Fry in Homer, they change

the oil often: and this fellow I met in a
factory once told a joke in which a guy sticks

up his middle finger to this lady and says,
check your oil? that is not very nice: I

mean, what could he do for her: just say,
lady, your oil's fine: because what if it

wasn't, could he replenish a drought: my
father's friend once said he needed to "grease

his axle": I think that was a dirty expression:
if not dirty, brutally suggestive and insulting,

and take that little gland in the reproductive
works of human males, the one that puts out a

bead of oil to promote penetration: tell me,
is that not as wonderful as an appearance in a

grotto: how did "myself" know that some
problem outside my body might arise that a

gland should be designed to help ease: a gland
in me to help me ease in her: take anything,

think about it, it blows up in wonder: now, I
can't call this greaseshooter dirty, it's so

splendid, but I don't want anything to do with
it: I would rather think about the girl's

collarbone than that and that bone: I just
tell you, it's amazing: then, there's oil and

vinegar, oilcloth, etc. but

THAT'S OIL, FOLKS

America

Eat anything: but hardly any: calories are
calories: olive oil, chocolate, nuts, raisins

—but don't be deceived about carbohydrates
and fruits: eat enough and they will make you

as slick as butter (or really excellent cheese,
say, parmesan, how delightful): but you may

eat as much of nothing as you please, believe
me: iceberg lettuce, celery stalks, sugarless

bran (watch carrots, they quickly turn to
sugar): you cannot get away with anything:

eat it and it is in you: so don't eat it: &
don't think you can eat it and wear it off

running or climbing: refuse the peanut butter
and sunflower butter and you can sit on your

butt all day and lose weight: down a few
ounces of heavyweight ice cream and

sweat your balls (if pertaining) off for hrs
to no, I say, no avail: so, eat lots of

nothing but little of anything: an occasional
piece of chocolate-chocolate cake will be all

right, why worry: lightning-lit, windswept
firelines scythed the prairies and strung

rivers of clearing through the hardwoods,
disaster renewal, smallish weeds and bushes

getting their seeds out, grazing attracting
rabbits and buffalo, the other big light

shining in steady. . . .

In View of the Fact

The people of my time are passing away: my
wife is baking for a funeral, a 60-year-old who

died suddenly, when the phone rings, and it's
Ruth we care so much about in intensive care:

it was once weddings that came so thick and
fast, and then, first babies, such a hullabaloo:

now, it's this that and the other and somebody
else gone or on the brink: well, we never

thought we would live forever (although we did)
and now it looks like we won't: some of us

are losing a leg to diabetes, some don't know
what they went downstairs for, some know that

a hired watchful person is around, some like
to touch the cane tip into something steady,

so nice: we have already lost so many,
brushed the loss of ourselves ourselves: our

address books for so long a slow scramble now
are palimpsests, scribbles and scratches: our

index cards for Christmases, birthdays,
Halloweens drop clean away into sympathies:

at the same time we are getting used to so
many leaving, we are hanging on with a grip

to the ones left: we are not giving up on the
congestive heart failure or brain tumors, on

the nice old men left in empty houses or on
the widows who decide to travel a lot: we

think the sun may shine someday when we'll
drink wine together and think of what used to

be: until we die we will remember every
single thing, recall every word, love every

loss: then we will, as we must, leave it to
others to love, love that can grow brighter

and deeper till the very end, gaining strength
and getting more precious all the way. . . .

Get Over It

I guess old men aren't really good for nothing:
they can cuddle, shuffle, and look

about for where it all went: harmless, they
are attractive, gently innocent, on park benches

or subways, or on the slow side of streets:
women are reassured by them; they are witnesses

without danger, guardian angels: out of the
game, earnings free, they are what they earned

before: they hardly compete at all: their toothless
mouths need no upkeep, no reconstructions,

no root canals or extraordinary measures:
it doesn't matter if their piss-burnt pants

stiffen up or if they seldom shave or use much
hot water: they are wonderfully inexpensive:

unless, of course, something goes wrong: they
just hang out on corners or in alleys, useless,

apologetic, inexcusable, supernumerary,
invisible among the seeing: what good is a mess

of stuff on its way out, nearly out: get on
out, you might say, you're taking up room:

but old men are good examples to the young of
what becomes of things: working, loving,

buying, living the dynamics, many can look
down the steep gradient of the slope to where

the rubbish edges the river and then reaffirmed
they can look back into the lights and run

along to do their parts: when I started this
piece, I intended under the guise of praise

to pour the world's contempt on old men, but
I wasn't clever enough to modulate it gradually

the way, say, Shakespeare moves easefully
through changing weathers: but at times, old

men will look up at the world, raise an eyebrow
and smile a small smile hard to read.

Tail Tales

Old men drain and dread and dream and dress
and dribble and drift and drink and drip and

drone and drool and droop and drop and drown
and drowse, dry, and dry up: I won't show my

obvious hand and do anymore with this: I can't
stand to be noticed for just carrying something

out: except, of course, at a carry-out or if
the chamber pot needs to be carried out: but,

I mean, just to do something, without the risk
of running into breaks, barricades, burdens

or barristers—what lift can such drudgery
sustain, no, what lift can sustain such

drudgery: I was scanning the other day when
I hit on this show with Alan Brinkley: I

liked him so much, I went to the bookstore to
get a book but all they had was the one on

the New Deal, which I didn't care for—I
wanted to read him on something slightly more

philosophical, summary, or theoretical: but
he was so quick to catch on (not that it's

probably that hard to outgrasp Schlesinger or
Galbraith) and he understood the other points

of view better than the other points of view
did but still didn't like them, didn't prefer

them to his own: well, you can see, if you
add insight, gentleness, evidence to all that

why I would get interested: I'm sure I
demonstrate in my own practice a sheer flow of

the viable juice, so no wonder I recognize a
river of it in another: not that antiquity

has perjured sense in S & G: they cut about
them smartly: really valuable old men. . . .

Fuel to the Fire, Ice to the Floe

In knee boots men work at the street grilles
to plunge flow through the leaves plugging the

storm drains: what I mean is, it rained a lot
and you know when it does autumn leaves wash

down the runoff and get stuck in the drains,
plug up the drains till the water backs up

and elongates lakes along the street or fits
nicely into concrete-boundaried corners: but

if the language doesn't caper or diddle, who
cares what the water does or if the men get in

over their boots: I have the same clogging
problems with my gutterspouts (among other

things): this guy put in a sieve to keep the
leaves out of the pipe when the opaque sieve

reduced the flow to zero and the gutters
overspilled: I am a patient man and can—

though just barely—afford some experimentation
but after a while I'd just as soon move somewhere

else, Arizona or the Sahara: I just can't
take it when things do not go right, although

I patiently grit my teeth and persist in calm:
trouble is it all breaks out at night, some

kind of itching or bowel contraction or loose
saliva: anyway, it seemed like a poetic

thing to think of, the men in their yellow
raingear and black hipboots looking down

trying to find an open bottom to a pond, with
it still raining, etc., you know.

Suet Pudding, Spotted Dick

All well and good for autonomy that it find
its way into the full array of itself—good

or evil: that it achieve (whether poem or
self) whatever standing defense can carve out

of imposition or inner resources can assert:
but what of it if one thing, uncompromised,

unassaulted by the world's mixtures, stands
out alone in the glorious testament of itself:

what good is it if it cannot bend to use:
is being, however fully realized, enough: one

can be in oneself alone and each of us must,
of necessity, so be alone each in the measure

of himself: but only when one's self engages
other selves does whatever is apply: and what

will application (wyrcan) to search out among
the diversities of others a riding autonomy:

an autonomy that will ride over, do what it
can, invoke, say, justice, liberty, wellbeing

for all (or many, or as many as possible,
some?): hidden by leaves on the limber end

of a twig all summer, the hornet's nest is now, after
fall, the only thing in the tree: except for

a scrap of leaves blown in from the oak close
by: but where are the hornets, are they in

there: is there more endangerment in summer
than winter notice: I hope the plague of the

bee mites will pass this year: I sure did
miss the bees, the honeybees, the flower people.

Focal Lengths

I'm largely a big joke: if somebody else
doesn't make a crack about me, I do: the

burn center in me is too steady a place to
dwell in: I go by there, throw rocks, and

laugh my head off when the windows splinter:
kaplooey: what kind of little nerd is doing

a little serious reading in there: what is
this, a library: then, I roar: all that

faked up type lining shelves like boot camp
drills: what does it have to do with anything:

did I take my bristled nest of humiliations
to heart: what kind of dunce keeps a fire

going like this: what do people mean coming
to hell to warm themselves: well, it *is*

warm: the fire, stoked by whatever, is truly
burning: so, that's the way I am: I just

can't keep it straight: people melt down in
the heat sometimes and weep: I just don't

know what to do: I just jump-start my pickup
and drive off: I just declare to goodness:

but I know something about burning, myself:
better laugh it off: better not believe it:

better not think it's real: it's not real:
it's so cool: actually, it's nothing: it's just

nothing: crack it up: make it go away.

Sibley Hall

The gingko's so all-gold you want to put it in
the bank, but the beautiful young girl having

her sandwich on the steps of the art building
said to me, it loses all its leaves at once:

so much gold!

Good God

It used to flick up so often, I called it
flicker: but now, drooping, it nods awake

or, losing it, slips back asleep: I say,
stand up there, man, but, you know, it's only

me, and it takes no threat to heart, so to
speak: it's lazier than a sick dog that won't

lift his head to sniff the wind: it has
always amused me as a serviceable irony that

the spirit, which is without substance, can
move the flesh: a thought, a sight, a scent

frizzing the wires of the mind (sounds like
substance) and the thing, you know the thing,

just reacts, warms, fills, lengthens, hardens
without hands or lips, without touch: so we

must think of the spirit as a matter of great
force and be mindful that while it works it

works wondrously but later on in life, say,
the spirit may be willing and the flesh weak,

as you've heard said: you could suppose the
spirit at that point *not very willing* or it

could come up with something: or perhaps the
thing, long asleep, has fallen out of use: a

day of radical separation, a realization that
puts you back before the world began—alone:

the walls of the grave your only embrace, and
the soil you lie on all that lies on you: my

goodness: fortunately, there are remedies—
implants, injections, dirty magazines: the

world is sometimes so well provided with 2nd
or 3rd chances, we must be amazed at the

thoughtfulness of so many applied to so wide
a scope of possibility and give the pisspoor

thing a chance. . . .

Genetic Counseling

You know how babies in kindergarten catch (or
give) a new cold every week, and how young

people in college, you see their breakfast or
lunch spilled by the walkways, or you see them

flash down the hall loaded with a bathroom
urgency: it's because these new people, their

flexibility is so wide they have to take on
the definitions of immunity, and their bowels

have to adjust to the environmental influx:
gradually, they settle in: you sometimes see

old folks cold-free and nicely trained for yrs
at a time; they and not-they have fought out

a partial standoff allowing lingering peace:
young people are green, tender, responsive &

so delightful (usually): it takes time for
them to become anything you can count on: I'm

glad I can put, with all this talk, slosh back
into the metrically-induced compressions of

terrorist tightwads who've squeezed the
tradition so lean so long: these neat little

packets of considered richness, excluding the
wasted grandeur of dull prairies and empty

seas, so much ice plunging off Antarctica,
these little tightly packed exclusions, what,

is't not nobler and more a liking of the maker
to sprinkle hedgerows up and down anything,

repeat krill astonishingly, fill up a sky with
rolling rows of discrete white clouds (imagine

what it would cost!), what's the matter with
dirt, dirt, and more dirt, and a little bit

more: can one be big and rich: but what about
the poor patch where only perking geysers can

cough up a little green: oh, don't mess with
me: do I have to tell you everything. . . .

Hooliganism

Once (there was a time when) I was attracted
to, if not attractive to, everybody, starlet

and streetlet, athlete and bellybag: afire,
I burned anything, including myself: kneedeep

in ashen brush, even some simmering fagots, I
tried to separate the heat from the flame but

gave up, pouring it all into the love of a wife
now nearly half a century old—the wife a

little older: most of those old flames (sweet
people) have flickered away except for the

corner of my mind where lively they live on in
honor, honorary doctorates circling their

laureled heads—what schools they founded!
taking what pains, with what tears, they taught

me how, roaring possibilities and tenderest
glows: love, love, one learns to love, it is

not easy, yet not to love, even astray, leaves
something left for the grave: burnt out

completely is ease at last, the trunk honeyed
full as a fall hive: when the light dies out

at last on the darkening coals, the life
turns to jewels, so expensive, and

they never give the sparkle up: this was
a fancy, and not half fancy enough and somewhat

lacking in detail but ever true.

Slacking Off

You don't put them in, they can't stay in:
calories, I mean: you don't put them in, you

don't have to get them out: you can sit all
day at the TV, a couch potato, and shrivel up like

a stale french fry: you won't have to exercise
a bit, pretty soon a skeleton would look fat

next to you: that's a skeleton that died of
thick bones from too much exercise: who won't

get close enough to the edge of definition
won't get the edge in "living on the edge":

why won't some come to edges others can't keep
away from: answer me that: okay, I'll do it:

if your differentiation, so-called, is a
similitude broadly applying why then your

identity dissolves in happy safety with the
group, crowd, nation, even continent, unless

you're away, say out of town or away on business
or vacation: then you might find you had

transported your singular distinction into the
midst of a major otherness: mostly, though,

as you would probably want to get on back home
you would warmly and wholeheartedly identify

with your likenesses or kind: if your
differentiation is poorly peopled, you may

rub the majority abrasively, and it may be
dangerous for you to show your face or unwind

your genome: better keep your mouth shut,
unless you can represent the growing edge of a

coming time when, it may be, you can move more
smoothly in and out of the circuits of grace:

but if you come clean as an abomination, better
snitch a helicopter and get the fuck out: the

animals, you know, other than ourselves though
much the same, are like archeological sites:

we need to plunder their behavior to get at the
roots and devices pertaining to survival on

this planet: the lions, how they interact,
killing, eating, mating, their disputes among

themselves: and the orang-utans, our motives
written simply, deeply, silently: even the

bacteria, little hordes swimming this way and
that together: a piece of fossil notable in

me says hit it, git it, and git: but, of
course, that looks out of place dragged out in

front of our cultural conditioning. . . .

Quibbling the Colossal

I just had the funniest thought: it's the
singing of Wales and whales that I like so

much: you know, have you heard those men's
groups, those coal miners and church people in

Wales singing: to be deeply and sweetly undone,
listen in: and the scrawny risings and

screechings and deep bellowings of whales,
their arias personal (?) and predatory at

love and prey—that makes up mind for us as
we study to make out mind in them: the reason

I can't attain world view or associational
complexity is that when I read I'm asleep by

the second paragraph: also, my poems come in
dislocated increments, because my spine between

the shoulderblades gets to hurting when I type:
also, my feet swell from sitting still: but

when the world tilts one way it rights another
which is to say that the disjunctiveness of my

recent verse cracks up the dark cloud and
covering shield of influence and lets fresh

light in, more than what little was left, a
sliver along the farthest horizon: room to

breathe and stretch and not give a shit, room
to turn my armies of words around in or camp

out and hide (bivouac): height to reach up
through the smoke and busted mirrors to clear

views of the beginnings high in the oldest
times: but seriously you know, this way of

seeing things is just a way of seeing things:
time is not crept up on by some accumulative

designer but percolates afresh every day like
a hot cup of coffee: and, Harold, if this is

an Evening Land, when within memory was it
otherwise, all of civilized time a second in

the all of time: good lord, we're all so
recent, we've hardly got our ears scrubbed,

hair unmatted, our teeth root-canaled: so,
shine on, shine on, harvest moon: the computers

are clicking, and the greatest dawn ever is
rosy in the skies.

CAST THE OVERCAST

Informing Dynamics

We don't live near a stream, but now we do:
the water slipping down the side of the street

would shame many a river with a big name
inscribed on space shots, with a history, with

fish: three or four inches this morning and
more coming: a flotation medium rising in the

basement, alas, a mop and bucket my squeezing
remedy: and Phyllis is off at a funeral:

put down in this much water, one could drown;
at least, get wet: but what does the body

care that has no spirit in it: it has already
drowned in a medium sleep pales before: and

the spirit, even: it was just a bit of
electricity firing off joints and nets: off,

it isn't there anymore: the body, though, is
but it has taken on the temperature of the

ground and sees no difference in itself: oh,
but the difference to some! a lifetime's

worth of getting on with life: it is just that
quick cut between getting our monographs

published about horse fever and keeping the drain
free below the rainspout and putting a little

aside for the kids' education and—BOP—gone:
I have so much trouble with that edge: the

day-to-day plunged into eternity: the look
back then from eternity to the day-to-day:

what was it all about, what was the use, how
did we get so interested, so worried, so

anxious: I say, meaning cannot be criticized
by time: where does time get off: while there

is meaning, there is meaning: meaninglessness
is not the opposite but the absence of

meaning: when anything has served its purpose
it might as well be abandoned, even meaning:

but meaning is really good while it lasts: too
bad you can't store it up anywhere for a download.

Pyroclastic Flows

I'm on drugs, now: this is the way people on
too much medicinal uplift write: they are

very nearly sorry that they cannot take you
very seriously: they have been rendered

incapable of their own tragedy: they don't
understand how anyone can hold a strong opinion

or crave a stiff measure: they are the first
to hold themselves up to the mirror of

inconsequence and smile: they don't grasp
that their ribbons are on a flogging stick:

I say to the man, are you my provider: when
I need the feelings, I get down on my knees

and say, wipe out some of the darkness, put the
jiggle back in: how much is that: the druggist

flips out his counting knife and 5, 10, 15,
there they go, one a day, twice if need be,

only as prescribed: well, it takes a few wks
of flushing and burning to get on them but

then you cool out, you float, you are under
the wings of butterflies: the air, you know,

is not just nothing: it is a medium like the
sea but thinner: things, as fishes in water

do, float in it—mites, and household plants
called yeasts, sundry viral and bacterial

organisms: you've seen pictures of those big
catfish breathing thick water: well, we have

our own strainers, blockers, and sort of gills:
already here 70 years, I don't get too shook

up about what floats in the air: as long as
it's not me or only my drugs, honey

HARD ASSETTE

Odd Man Out

I'm just an old man in a de-gilded (gelded?) cage: a
bird, too: I think I'm a hornbill: when I

blow hard, I get a horny sound: it whacks
off tree trunks: my friends in the forest

want to know what's the fuss about: frankly,
I can't keep it down: I try to hum a lot

instead and look way out into the periphery:
but as to a lodestone or couple of lodestones

my attention wanders back and seizes exigency
out of aura: listen, talk about old: mineral

deposits stiffen old men's bladder walls: at
the latrine, if you can get started, only,

say, the first level, a third, goes, especially
if you're in a hurry: you cut it off: the

walls, you know, need to collapse to the
remaining quantity: that takes time: you

could shake away with a bladder hardly spent:
old men have to stand there and soon they can

feel the second level acquire pressure, and
then when they get down to the last dribble

there's probably half a pint unencircled: we,
you, they have to work at it: but out in the

forest meanwhile the monkeys burble, the floor
viper slides: give it half an hour, then

RAISE A BEAD

Squall Lines

They say of us old people, look, what do you
care, how much do you have to lose: go ahead,

cruise down the Volga and check out Petersburg
or drive into New York City: if you get

blipped off, what's that: it won't be long
before you blip off anyhow: why, what has a

25-year-old built up in 25 years that compares
with a 70-year-old's trove: think of the

perspective, the seasoning, the long loves,
the vigil till enemies die: also, how about

the money, prestige, the real estate: what,
you ask, do the old have to lose, why, more &

more till sitting back in easy splendor they
don't want to go at all: but the 25-year-old

will complain that if he flips he loses what
he had yet to gain: still wet behind the ears

he doesn't even know what that is (not that
anyone does): alas, the old have little in

that bank: the young inherit the world, but
we already have it, except we've had it. . . .

John Henry

This morning I greeted my wife's waking with
how's my little dewberry but, poor thing, the

answer was a rotten sore throat, headache,
   upset stomach and, soon determined, 100.2

fever: so I said to her, well, there you are:
sometimes these berries mold or canker on the

vine: an oblong aspirin, coke (potable), half
a slice of toast, and cuddled up in a corner

of the couch with the Ithaca Journal and the
Wall Street Journal she is locating, I hope,

the road to recovery: but that hacking cough:
dry, unyielding, nothing getting up: feathers:

this train has run out of track pppsssssstttt. . . .

Rogue Elephant

The reason to be autonomous is to stand there,
a cleared instrument, ready to act, to search

the moral realm and actual conditions for what
needs to be done and to do it: fine, the

best, if it works out, but if, like a gun, it
comes in handy to the wrong choice, why then

you see the danger in the effective: better
then an autonomy that stands and looks about,

negotiating nothing, the supreme indifferences:
is anything to be gained where as much is lost

and if for every action there is an equal and
opposite reaction has the loss been researched

equally with the gain: you can see how the
milling actions of millions could come to a

buzzard-like glide as from a coincidental,
warm bottom of water stuck between chilled

peaks: it is not so easy to say, okay, go on
out and act: who, doing what, to what or

whom: just a minute: should the bunker be
bombed (if it stores gas): should all the

rattlers die just because they rattle: if I
hear the young gentleman vomiter roaring down

the hall in the men's room, should I go and
inquire of him, reducing him to my care: no

wonder the great sayers (who say nothing) sit
about in inaccessible states of mind: no

wonder still wisdom and catatonia appear to
exchange places occasionally: but if anything

were easy, our easy choices soon would carry
away our ignorance with the world—better

let the mixed up mix and let the surface shine
with all the possibilities, each in itself.

Mouvance

Hilarity and sour scorn typify my reactions to
passions of the moment: I mean, seeing people

expend themselves into fugitive extremes, it
speaks poorly of the power of the mind to

govern any kind of distances: until you
consider that passions, except in intense

subduals too longrange to bear, only come in
moments, so if you are to get any passion out

of life, you'll have to dig it out of narrow
spaces or squeeze all you have into slender,

if deep, circumstance: I myself have never
known what to do about anything: as I look

back, I see not even a clown but a clown's
clothes flapping on the clothesline of some

tizzy: is it really wise so to anticipate
and prepare for the storm, so to gauge it in

terms of other storms, that when the fierce
lightning breaks and high wind falls blunt

against you you just look away with a numb
nonchalance: what about the splintering free

of the green branches, the bubbly pelt and
spray of windy rain on sudden pools, what

about the vigorous runaway of rivulets finding
themselves: what, what, did not the vibrance

of the ground in that thud click your teeth:
think of the tranquillity, all passion spent,

when the passion passes and you lie back in
a relief of sweet feeling: whereas, unspent

you would just growl your away into the next
worry of the next storm: hark, the bells are

ringing, the announcements are in preparation,
might as well start singing. . . .

Called Into Play

Fall fell: so that's it for the leaf poetry:
some flurries have whitened the edges of roads

and lawns: time for that, the snow stuff: &
turkeys and old St. Nick: where am I going to

find something to write about I haven't already
written away: I will have to stop short, look

down, look up, look close, think, think, think:
but in what range should I think: should I

figure colors and outlines, given forms, say
mailboxes, or should I try to plumb what is

behind what and what behind that, deep down
where the surface has lost its semblance: or

should I think personally, such as, this week
seems to have been crafted in hell: what: is

something going on: something besides this
diddledeediddle everyday matter-of-fact: I

could draw up an ancient memory which would
wipe this whole presence away: or I could fill

out my dreams with high syntheses turned into
concrete visionary forms: Lucre could lust

for Luster: bad angels could roar out of perdition
and kill the AIDS vaccine not quite

perfected yet: the gods could get down on
each other; the big gods could fly in from

nebulae unknown: but I'm only me: I have 4
interests—money, poetry, sex, death: I guess

I can jostle those. . . .

Back-Burnerd

No sooner do I say I don't do something than I
do: no sooner do I say I believe something

than I don't: the minute something comes up
clear, behind me it goes: it no longer seems

to be surrounding: it wasn't till I saw it
that I saw it was a basket or bucket not big

enough to hold enough: and anyhow when
one is in the habit of looking for something

how do you find something to do after you've
found something, why, look for something else:

I guess we're pushed ahead into what we call
progress, hoping: I'm soaring today like a

dead mole: I have as much get up and go as a
rock bottom: the point of it all has folded

back into a parachute drag: the narrative
has cracked, too brittle for bridges:

my father, begetting my coming hither, begat
my leave: my mother bore me between two legs

but hence between twelve I will slowly go:
there's nothing like nothing on a hungover

morning: they say: I don't drink: it's
just that phrases come to me: I think, what

can I do with this: into the trash, a possibility:
but I'm a saver, I hold on: having something

to hold on to for an old man, even if it's like
a turkey snood or slack eelette, is better

than a smooth cutoff of things: we must not
leave the hapless helpless hopeless: who

knows when the next beautiful morning will
appear: for sure. . . .

A Few Acres of Shiny Water

I guess anything gets old: being rich, yep,
pretty soon it's old—occasional pleasant

spurts of realization, then—celebrity, a big
ox in your way wherever you turn, that gets

old: having nothing to do gets old in a hurry,
going from having something to do to not being

able to find anything to do, I'll say: being
in love, oh, dear, even that, about the third

month, gets old as hell, all those re-arisings:
on the bestseller list—great the first week,

also the second week; then it's every week,
expected, tedious, getting old: market up,

wow, up again, oh, boy, still up, up and up,
I see, okay, really: you are finally thought

to be as good a poet as you thought—so; so
what, what is a poet: even getting old gets

old, the novelty aches and pains, surprising
and scary at first, they don't wear off but

the novelty does: finding, and trying to
find, something new gets old: find a new

risk to take, a new cliff to sail off from,
pretty soon it's a drag to get all the way to

Nepal or a Filipino trench: telling about
getting old and everything getting old gets

old, I'll tell you, it sure does. . . .

"They said today would be partly cloudy"

They said today would be partly cloudy: I'd
like to see the other part: this part is

clearly apparent, which is to say, cloudy:
alas, that ever flakes were snow: the effect

of lake effect snow is in dawn's early light
about five inches, the plows not out, the

birds not singing, the muffled night turned
to bleached silence: but what do we here

expect, why, this: but a partly day promised,
this whole one so far is flurried: have

you ever thought how the weather, of which
there is such a tedious plenty, especially

when nothing happens for months, say, no rain
or no sun, have you ever thought how the

weather is just the planet carrying on, an
atmospheric thing native to these millions

of turnings in space: I mean, that it has
no reference to us: the weather is its weather:

it doesn't even know that the roads are slick
or deep or that the hill roads are sliding

passageways into ditches and brambles: it
isn't aware that someone is tangled in a

drift or that a big drift is sliding down on
someone: it's just amazing how much it doesn't

know: it doesn't know anything.

Feint Praise

The world has dealt (nothing personal)
outrageously with me: now, I deal back: it's

like arguing with the head-chopper, though, where can
it get me: I guess I could get to where I'd

be saying, look, sir, do you fully realize what
you're doing: is there any room for

negotiation here, like, your head or mine:
(when an artist, say, striving to be normal,

isn't, there you have genuine stuff: not
necessarily the best stuff: but, how much

better to replace the unachievable with the
inadvertent: this is what an artist means

when he says he's not responsible for his
genius, it just happens: but, alas, if the

artist quite normal enough strives to be
weird, the shocking falsity wears so thin a

sheen it's soon hardly shocking and far more
dismissible:) (the material in the preceding

parenthesis is worth thinking on): (to go the
other way further out into the periphery is

to lose hold on the central issues and
become thin, manneristic, too arty, and

mere).

Surfacing Surface Effects

A small moon nearly melted in the almost-morning
night, I arise and thank God I can get up:

(we used to use paper napkins but lately my
wife has taken to pulling upscale cloth napkins

through wooden rings but since we don't want
to soil the cloth napkins, we now have no

napkins at all): dawn turns the moon into a
crust of bumpy ice, and I go out paled by

reality to face the world, the world again,
still there (thank goodness, but still there):

the smallest crevices and narrowest alleyways
of pleasure microscopic nearly in the wide

blank recalcitrance, a scope: (the weatherman
said he would give us the causes of the changes

in the weather when what we wanted was

CHANGES IN THE CAUSES)

Free One, Get One By

I'm over and done with: disengaged, I'm up
for grabs: if you want me, you can have me,

floating: I'm useless to any use; having none, ready for
any direction: (this is not

exactly the way I heard myself saying this
on the way to the typewriter: the first

part sounds right, but then something ever so
slightly fancy feeds a little rot in—oh, but

that reminds me, one of the urinals at the
university is out of order and a blank sheet

has been hung over it saying OUT OF ORDER but
I think some leftover piss, hidden in there,

has rotted: so I was thinking yesterday
of ROTTEN PISS: imagine, rotten piss: even

that rots—and smells: stinks: stand next
to it, it cuts your breath off (and your piss)

one knows, of course, what things come to, an
end, bobbing free, fortunately, in

when: one on the row, say, wouldn't want a
definite date, would he (she): but how rude

to have the head man just walk in on you,
possibly in your underwear, and say, hurry up:

please, it's time: what, no time to lift off
the prepared speeches like balloons, airy

forms fingering the precincts of heaven for
mercy: mercy, mercy: what could one do then

but cast off into terror and restraint as
filling as any significant finish: over and

done with, available to the stars, one
has no further use for oneself, all that

remains is to smell. . . .

THANK YOU FOR YOUR COOPERATION

Dumb Clucks

Up, O Nothing, where the coming together of
everything ends everything, the aboriginal

emptiness, source of all beginnings, where
spirit at last totally prevails, up there,

this awing site the brain sees, does it need
a universe to back it up and, if not, is it

anything but a wisp, or are universe and wisp,
one and another kind of disappearance again

all one: who cares: here, one is wed to two
and the outbreak of things into sweetness and

pain binds and frees us: what, after all, is
greater than the toe of a child, and does any

truth supercede a gushingly ripe pear or
peach or collection of grape pulps: one's

fame in the hands of a reviewer is not so much
a spur as a poniard: it is seldom the case

that praise has so o'erswelled (o'erswollen)
one that the doctor prescribes daggers: one

sustains oneself on mice- and chickenfeed and
can be swept away in the wind of the slightest

disfavor: well, we are such dust as housemites
husband on, riding microscopic currents in the

stillest parlor air. . . .

UNSIGHTLY HAIR

Sucking Flies

No longer confident of the transfigurations, the
assemblages, piercing coordinations, the wound

unwound into a new winding wound again—now,
I just put in the wording: I give words to the

passing music, taking it as it is, where it goes:
who am I to prevail upon the shallows to reveal

their source materials, the hidden currents,
hidden drives (as the road signs say): what I

am not is a teacher: if Heraclitus, Aristotle,
Bacon, Burke have not taught the world then

teaching doesn't work, is not the issue: (but
the music gets so flat: the energies of

transforming lift up, tensely integrative, into
new formations young, beautiful: whereas,

merely to go along with scrambling mediocrity
is to defer too much to the world:) oh, how

flat it is (so much so that exclaiming about it
nearly gets a rise out of me): is disillusion

wise, or is it wise to fiddle with fragilities,
little dreams and hopes and foolish beliefs:

there is a smallness runs under things like a
crumbly soil that takes in what remains and

gives back the beauties of the field: our
bodies share these worm-shaken roads: but our

spirit, it is from before and knows no changes
through all the lineations of consequence. . . .

Balsam Firs

With my wife and me, it isn't so much that we
have used each other up—we really can't do

that—but that time has used us up: we stand
on the frail end of a long plank where things

get jittery and, because of the uncertainties,
almost new again: but time, time, has built

us so far out, we're nearly off the ship: we
turn to each other and say, look, there's

plenty here to do something about, but do you
suppose, so late, it's worth getting started:

still, life is now as it has always been, such
as it has been, life, and we say let's get on

with it: colloquial idioms at such times
soften sharpness—or, one might say, run an

iron rod out under the plank: I, myself, am
not much use: I have churned the word mill so

long that I can't pick out anything from
anything: I've said everything and mostly

cared when it sounded good: but my wife is as
solid as a jug or judge: her words, purporting

to mean, are bottom lines: I listen to her:
sometimes, I write down what she says, too:

but getting back to the boat, I'm for running
a few sails up and hooking into the changes:

we're feeling blustery and the open deep spills
out where the farthest sight is only sea. . . .

Tree-Limbs Down

The poverty of having everything is not
wanting anything: I trudge down the mall halls

and see nothing wanting which would pick me
up: I stop at a cheap $79 piece of jewelry,

a little necklace dangler, and it has a diamond
chip in it hardly big enough to sparkle, but it

sparkles: a piece of junk, symbolically vast;
imagine, a life with a little sparkle in it, a

little sparkle like wanting something, like
wanting a little piece of shining, maybe the

world's smallest ruby: but if you have everything
the big carats are merely heavy with price and

somebody, maybe, trying to take you over: the dull
game of the comers-on, waiting everywhere like

moray eels poked out of holes: what did Christ
say, sell everything and give to the poor, and

immediacy enters; daily bread is the freshest
kind: dates, even, laid up old in larders, are

they sweet: come off sheets of the golden
desert, knees weak and mouth dry, what would

you think of an oasis, a handful of dates, and
a clear spring breaking out from under some stones:

but suppose bread can't daily be found or no
oasis materializes among the shimmers: lining

the outside of immediacy, alas, is uncertainty:
so the costly part of the crust of morning

bread is not knowing it will be there: it has
been said by others, though few, that nothing

is got for nothing: so I am reconciled: I
traipse my dull self down the aisles of

desire and settle for nothing, nothing wanted,
nothing spent, nothing got.

Wetter Beather

When a person inquires too much into my
condition, I wonder if he searches for ill

or good: as for my typewriter, it will not do
well in a humidity, it takes on a gummy

lethargy, it refuses its spaces, stalling its
keys which, certainly, just fling themselves

idly against a nonchalance: but let a cool
front through or let a heat wave require the

air conditioner and the keys flick along as easily
as thought: this foreknowledge prevents me

from hastening off, heavy manual machine under
my arm or confined upon my hip by the arm,

hastening off, I say, to the repair shop—
a lucky patience because there no longer are

any shops for this device, and few ribbons
around and sparse typewriter paper: I am in

the midst of a technological redoing which
I will not abide till the radiant screens no

longer flicker: but my talent is so expired
that I need not trouble myself with digital

advances, I merely amuse myself in the comfort
of my own surrounding ignorance, with no

intention of publication and, of course, little
hope that others will press me thru the press.

The Gushworks

When what it was is what it is (or when what
it is is what it was) there you have an overlap:

for example, when you blow your nose, you
could, you know, close the handkerchief on the

product: instead, you are likely to open up
to see WHAT IT WAS: was it just a clear

gelatinous blob or a crusty skin shield or a
butterball of gooey glop: or as when you go

to the bathroom, you could flush before rising
but you probably rise before flushing: you

want to see WHAT IT WAS: you want to find out
if what it was going to be can be elicited

into a knowledge of what it now is: like an
oyster-type gob, your nose, I mean: I am a

member of the vertical circle whose arc passes
through a height above nearly all human interest

and whose depth encloses the silences of most
human shame: there is a sense in which the

integrity of the circle is taut throughout,
indifferent to its notches and degrees, as

indifferent as the discourses of my fellows
remain to me: think little of me, I will

think no less of you: the axle goes right
through my ears, and the merriment is in all

the go-round.

Body Marks

Nailing down the cause of anything is not easy:
you notice a prominent strand in the random

weave and think, well, that's probably it: but
that may be there just to mislead the born or

else it works only in association with a set
of subsets or sublineations and only expensive

time can rectify a balance out of that: I say
why is my hipbone flashing out each step down

my femur this morning when I walked less than
usual yesterday: well, too many stairs: well,

slept on that side all night: well, it's really
your colon hurting: what? well, remember

last night during that TV drama you had one
leg stretched out to the coffeetable too long:

that could have defined a warp in your bone
pain calls attention to: well, well: you've

(I've) probably hit on it: which would prove
it out this evening, hanging your leg up there

again or not: that is the question: when in
the second grade, cut on the playground, I,

playing hounds and fox (I was the fox, the slow
boys the hounds) skidded my left knee over the

spike of a buried stump, I got a 3 to 4 inch
slash and nearly passed out: I felt so

important, though: imagine being taken to a
doctor's office! and all the expensive stuff

was unwound and wound onto me, with taping
and splinting (I almost said splintering):

3 weeks off from school: stitches put in,
torn out by bending the knee, re-stitched, and

you know how it goes when you're eight: I'm
70 now, and I still can see little white

raisures where the stitches ripped free: you
could know me anywhere: talk about identity:

I'm nobody else except myself, unless somebody
has a mark just like mine (backed up by

another scar (I won't tell you about now) on
the inside of my left wrist, not an attempt

at anything self-critical:) I'm sure you think
all this is just as important and worthy of

posterity as I do. . . .

Yonderwards

I want to do a painting: I want to slur a raw
shoulder: I want to bruise a man, look into

a woman's eyes you could travel through
for life as through a galaxy or toward one:

I want paint painting-through rubs out: how
about a sudden lush bush on the right hand side

with a distant small bridge topping it: and
from right top to left bottom a sweep (maybe

water) quickly broadening down: but then a
goat's head is right up front, on this side of

the river (?) and when you look away and look
back it is all a beautiful woman; perhaps, her

bosom is the moon filling the upper left hand
beyond the river: I want a painting to do me

in: I want to wilt down and supremely recover:
but look what happened to Ozymandias and

EVEN SHELLEY

Depressed Areas

It is one thing to be nobody, but to be nobody
in the South! there is no roping in the rope

ladder and there are no steps in the step: or
you're let to climb up high enough that a

missing rung will de-characterize your mounting:
or something pressured by your step will fly

up and pop you in the face: the blast will
bust your ast: but if by any vine-swinging

you cling on above the pitfalls and call out,
look, it's me, I'm way up—why the South will

notice its allowances credited you and now you
"owe something back"—the old give-back back

again: whereas out West the roads are longer
than the wanderers and up north in the City

the homeless sit out among the tall buildings
as noticeable and anonymous as Exxon: (if you

own a little Exxon, no hard feelings): but
who cares, poetry is like a swamp, it will make

up anywhere there's a bottom: and the great
trees after all whose tops only the sky can

see . . . they topple and the water eats them up:
what do you do when the metaphors are shaping

up to oppose your case: why, end the poem.

Dishes and Dashes

I always wanted (when I was a boy—and even
now) to have a stretch of water, at least a

farm pond or house pond, a little circular
flat thing with fish in it, pike and bream,

sunflowers: something glassy as the sky, that
could fill up with clouds (cloud and could)

that would crash into the banks where among the
sedges and grasses mosquito hawks and dragonflies

would pitch and tilt: the sheen and silver,
the stillness, a patch of lilies maybe, or a

clutch of cattails a redwing might get close
enough to jeer in: but I still have the sky,

deeper than any stillness I could get water to
hold, and the years go by and it clears blue

and breezy: the geese seesaw back and forth,
talking through: (neither a sayer nor a doer

be: be a beer (nonalcoholic)): much of my
sin is not original: a little verbal abuse

(herein demonstrated), a little self-abuse
(which I make a practice of keeping to myself):

a few painful exaggerations and oversights
(lies), etc., a fairly normal menu: more

nearly original are things like being part of
the web of human relations, wherein, for

example, we used to be tobacco growers, and
my mother, a religious person, hated tobacco

anyhow, but it would have killed her to know
she was killing people, something not known

way back then: but I, I brought the green
leaves up from the field by a Silver-drawn

sled, poor mule: but lately I advised a man
to stop smoking, *and he did*, but he gained

twenty pounds and ran into diabetes and high
blood pressure: put that in your pipe and

—no, no: that's what I mean: get down
on your knees and ask to be excused because

there isn't a damn thing you can do about much
of the damage you do: pray, brother, pray,

and join the praying crowd. . . .

Auditions

So there we were eating feathered dinosaur
meat for Sunday dinner and expecting the

return of Jesus Christ any minute: *looking
forward* to the return when, by the way, highly

disturbing reorientations would be invoked:
graves we had held still with rows of clam

shells would blast open and actual grandmothers
and grandpappies would flare up midair in musty

spiritual clothes and go off with the Lord: &
others of us, some in overalls, some in

sack-print dresses, would just be given the old
go-ahead: nobody left behind to look after the

little dinosaur biddies or Silver, poor
thing, shut up braying and whinnying in the

stable: the certainty of all this seemed to
me, even as a kid woozy on the edge of question,

to sort poorly with the advisability: I didn't
care that much, though, about disrupting

farming: good Lord, worming tobacco, digging
up manure, lugging slops: (October is a

lost April): (a matter of leaves, coming
green or going gold, leaves and comings): I

was so full of poetry this morning, the rose
leaves of the maple tree reflected by the

rising light back onto the hardwood floors, and
stuff, I starved myself at the piano with a

haunting tune (of my own composition) and that
just about brought tears to my wife's eyes,

and she was all the way back in the bathroom
fixing up to go off to the Farmers' Market:

but there is the frost on the ground: who can
be rich, really, except in grief, water turned

against everything it nourished, the sweet
fluid become splintery, furry with death-

spicules: the big chrysanthemum bunch,
somewhat compromised, the hanging impatiens,

shot (my floozy neighbor said, impatiens is
not *gardening*), the nasturtiums, really worse

off: but the fire bushes, the flame bushes,
have you noticed them: when the chlorophyll

goes, a red redder than the reddest rose
burns them up! how exciting, how like the

world's brightest fucking blood: sensual
grief: the old cliches of time: time that

seems so insubstantial, so weightless, how can
it haul so much stuff off, where are the

grappling hooks, the sliders and rollers, the
lifters and blowers-away, alas.

Between Each Song

I once would have said my sister Vida but now
I can just say my sister because the other

sister is gone: you didn't know Mona, lovely
and marvelous Mona, so you can't feel the

flooded solar plexus that grips me now: but
you may know (I don't know if I hope you will

or hope you won't—tossups between having and
holding) but you may know someone of your own

I don't quite know the pang for as you do: I
know but don't believe Mona is gone: she is

still so much with me, I can hardly tell I lost
anything when I lost so much: love is a very

strange winding about when it gets lost in
your body and especially when it can't find

the place to go to, the place it used to find: Mona is
in my heart in a way that burns my chest until

my eyes water: are you that way: even in the
midst of business I could think of caring for

you for that: but my sister Vida and I used
to have to daub (we called it dob) the baccer

barn: cracks between the uneven-log sides
had to be filled airtight with clay so the

furnace and flues could "cure" the tobacco
with slow, then high heat: we would dig a

bucket of clay from the ditch by the road
where streaks of white and red clay ran, add

water for a thick consistency, then climb the
rafters inside the barn and dob the cracks:

can you imagine: kids: (perhaps it beat
empty streets filled with drugs): I REALLY

THINK WE SHOULD GET IT OFF OR GET OFF IT

Mina de Oro

Old fools, you know, can't tell where they are
sometimes: they lose track of what is serious:

(when it comes to the stock market, I don't
count my chickens even *after* they hatch:

trends in the night can sweep the coops away:
excessive liquidity sloshes in great swells

around the planet, gullywashing some guys and
washing some others up onto the shores of

splendor: great mounds of money generated
from money, money free of any derivation from

commodity, can just send frail craft into a
tizzy of bobbing: but, of course, if you

catch a swell right and ride in with the combers
you can be deposited on material shore

safely): (but, you know, them brokers and
flimflam artists, them slick journalists and

fee seekers, they start up a wind, like a
typhoon of love of money (yo money), and the

liquidity break your dam down and wash all yo
money out in the street: you have to watch

them fasttalkers, they know what the weather's
like, and they changes it the way they want it:

put a little money in something conservative,
maybe a bond fund or a little bit of a stock

fund: how about a municipal: if you going to
branch out, get a little GE, a touch of AT&T,

and a couple of pharmaceuticals: look out for
them highflying IPO's and you better keep yo

mouth shut cause somebody gonna find out you
got a dollar left:) my father said one time

this old man lost his sow, she ran off, and
he saw her tracks where she trotted by this

old ditch: so he hid out behind some bushes
one evening and about dark he heard something coming

and when it got close he jumped out of the
bushes right onto the old sow's back, but it

turned out it was a bear, and the bear took
off, just lit out, don't you know: that's

what he said anyhow.

Widespread Implications

How sweetly now like a boy I dawdle by ditches,
broken rocky brooks that clear streams through

the golden leaves: the light so bright from
the leaves still up, scarlet screaming vines

lining old growths high or rounding domes of
sumac: how like a sail set out from harbor

hitting the winds I flounder this way and that
for the steady dealing in the variable time:

old boys are young boys again, peeing arcs
the pleasantest use of their innocence, up

against trees or into boles, rock hollows or
into already running water! returned from

the differentiation of manhood almost back to
the woman: attached but hinge-loose, flappy,

uncalled for and uncalled, the careless way
off into nothingness: where, though, but in

nothingness can the brilliance more brightly
abide, the ripple in a brook-warp as gorgeously

blank as a galaxy: I dropped the mouse,
elegantly supersmall, from the trap out by the

back sagebush, and all day his precious little
tooth shone white, his nose barely dipped in

blood: he lay belly up snow white in the
golden October morn, but this morning, the

next, whatever prowls the night has taken him
away, a dear morsel that meant to winter

here with us.

Above the Fray Is Only Thin Air

How do you account for things: take night
before last, a dry night, still, leaves from

the maple by the driveway worked a solid
semicircle on the driveway, really pretty but

thick: I raked it up in the afternoon: but
last night around midnight a drizzle that

turned slowly into a quiet rain started and
kept up till day and after day: but not more

than a few leaves fell, and plenty are still on
the tree: except right at the tip of some

branches, now stick sprays, where, by the way,
the hornets' nest rides right out in the open,

stiller than a balloon: but, I mean, why
didn't the weighted wet leaves come down, even

in bigger droves than on the dry night: my theory
founded on guesswork is that the dry night got

so dry it got crisp, and crisp cracked off the
stems from the branches: and so the leaves

just fell off: they didn't need any breeze or
rain: is that wonderful: do you suppose it's

so: who knows: maybe the night of the crisp
fall was really no more than a bear climbing

up there and shivering the tree, shaking them
down: I would just as soon know the answer to

some things as how a galaxy turns. . . .

Home Fires

I don't know how big I'll be tomorrow, you
know TOMORROW, but I wasn't much yesterday:

now I am more than I ever thought I would be
and that is fine with me, even if TOMORROW

I will be more (or less) because in many
pertinent ways I'll be far less TOMORROW than

I am today: know what I'm saying: I'm saying
it's okay: it is better to be first at the

finish line than finished at the first line
(tho that is hardly worse than last at the

last line, unless, of course, that's the
grave's rim, in which case one would not wish

to be first in any case, unless, as in some
natural disaster—an asteroid or an

artificial plane down—you might want to be
the first to go): if you go, here is a little

poem I have written for you . . .

Chez Vous

I don't
know

where you're
coming

from but
it's

no place
I

care to
visit

Pudding Bush Sopping Wet

Every now and then when I'm writing poetry I
decide to write a poem: here following is one

of my recent efforts:

Hierarchy

The lard
above,

the fat
guy,

the big
cheese

a poem repetition hampers: three times the
poem tries to get off, only to be hauled down

and started over, or continued in the same way:
but on the other hand that kind of repetitive

punching socks the point home: try another
one . . .

Nip Sipper

If you
stagger it

ought not
to be

just because
you're old

this one is, of course, very clever and
alludes to the history of western civilization

also to domestic abuse and also to persons
unmentionable in high office dealing with

significant affairs: but since my poems strive
to dislocate themselves from social affairs,

I play connections diffidently: it is
preferable to be an important poet by not

saying anything.

Spew

Somewhere out toward the tip of the downswinging
limberest limb the hornets attached their

sturdiest chance: so now the nest (not heavy
as a big mango which would crack off the branch)

like a paperlight airship bounds in the
thunderstorms but holds for the fair stillnesses:

(my point in all this is isn't it odd that the
hornets know to seek security (and safety) in

the most givingly insecure settings): (how &
whether to apply this to human affairs, who

knows how or whether): as for me turned out
to pasture like an old mule, I graze among the

skimpy thoughts for energy to keep me standing
up, however rickety, however far down the reach

to the little feed: I remember this farmer had
25 mules when tractors came along and the

stalls of the stable emptied and two tractors
sat there instead all winter, eating nothing:

except for one old stiff mule, Pet, she was:
they just let her out to graze, never to be

called for or hitched up again: I can see her
now nibbling out on a pasture rise and thinking

to myself well, there you are: here near the end of
August, my wife's hostas (as in, hosta la vista)

have spindled up into white shoots of bloom,
some opening, some open, some closing, a long

list of a serial event, so good for a cloudy
morning: I can't write any more "poems" like

this poem I'm writing: I've "done" too many
already: who dwelling over the WWW can find in

my poor pasture whatever but nettles, sourweed,
and an occasional chicken snake—

Vomit

When I went out in the dewy morning this
morning to see the hanging nasturtium, often

dry if it doesn't rain, there was a cool
cicada sitting right there inside the rim of

the pot: what, I said, and nudged him with my
pen, but I suppose not having been in song, he

was asleep or spent or dead, mercy: he looked
so big, the black-veined clear wings extending

behind him, but I just now went out there again,
say, noon, and he isn't there: I do hear a

cicada, though, up in a pine, I think, and it
may be he: or she: the sun is shining, the

front has passed through, the humidity has
dried up: it is at once cool and warm: I have

eaten a bellyful of fruit: also, a piece of
plaincake: when I am toothless, I shall recall

pound cake and milk: also hummus

Thoughts

I was reading in the *World Book* about A. E.
Housman wherein it was reported that he died
and was buried, so I said to myself, "Well,

Al, we know you're there, but you don't know
we're here," and that seemed to screw up the
strivings for immortality: no use to be

immortal in the bodies of others while one's
own body molds away or flakes off in pasty
chunks: this is a version of an old thought

of mine: one forgets before one is forgotten,
so don't worry about being remembered, just
worry about being, that's something to worry

about: so, Housey, I wish you could have
gotten what you wanted out of life: but the
other fellow had a right to get what he

wanted (or try to get what he wanted) out of
life, and since that wasn't what you wanted
well, there you go, but we know where you're at:

in fact, tho, A.E., you're not in your grave,
not the real you: whatever of the real you
is left is here with us: you're here with

us, in a sense: the grave holds nothing, or
what soon will be: but no one, now, dead or
alive can hold you in his arms and dry your eyes

Spit

Thinking I'd better be prepared when I went
out to meet the ocean, I blew myself up but

burst in time: so the next morning,
actually nearly before light, I converted

myself into a ghost crab, peeked out of my hole
over the sand, and there it was, the whole

wide thing, gray as the morning and on no
business but its own: when it washed over me

I waited, sealed off, underground until it
washed away: then I came out and the

ocean had become itself again: even so, the
sight burst my horizon: women's preferences

evolve the form of man, I'm told, a pretty
lousy trail of taste, the women apparently

wanting strength but not too much, independence
but heavily nurtured, paunches, wheezes, and

some broken-down feet: men, though, choose
women, too, but hardly a shriveled-up old

shrew or shrunken prune hasn't been fucked
over, over and over: the results lie and limp

in the streets: run-over heels and busted
belts decorate open air fashion: what went

wrong, you may ask: or is it right: why doth
perfection here and there in the wildest

statistic only appear: c'est la vie: yep:
something is more cockeyed than broad shouldered:

desire is the supreme beautician: she (or he)
deodorizes and/or fertilizes most any patch: he

(or she) rushes forward in her own perfection
till a port in some exigency (storm, I mean)

releases her to a free moment of disgust.

Lineage

Poets "say things": they shape stuff up and
make it "sound like something": it is shaping's

concision they're after, an airy framework
passing can pause in: though the framing and

passing are as if one: take pussy pussy, now:
that's p|-|uh|-|puh|-|sy poo-sy, puhsey poosy:

you know: pointing up separates out, limits
into identity: so, it's not poosy poosy, as

in calling your cat, or as in calling out at
night incoherently poosy poosy: no, it says

that the poosy is puhsy, though there may be
no such thing in the world but perfectly clean

sweet pussy: it is something we come into the
world through the back door of, a place dreams

and dreamers are made on, so tenderly secret,
so terrifying, gaunt, where I began, in fire,

which fled into windy air and lengthily slowed
and cooled into rain's fallen waters, running,

and then I became swamp or rockbottom ground:
what an old story, told only after the telling:

here now are the ceaseless maggots, the squirm
of disintegration, the obscene, vulgar, coarse,

the what-the-hell, beyond which, however, lies
the fire and dust, the refinements of

rebeginning: alas, that it could have been no
different until one sees it could have been

Now Then

You can have your bathroom window open an inch
and if the door is nearly closed, it can slam

it shut: the wind can: whereas, if the door
is standing open (as perhaps it shouldn't be)

(not if you're doing anything, you know, cool)
a hurricane would do little more than tremble

the door (however much it rattled the window);
may not, contrariwise, the physics be in the

metaphysics: which is to say that major effects
can come of slender spacings, while something

too wide open cannot be bothered by anything:
broadly, therefore, welcome the world, and if

you must have them keep your splinterings and
partitions solidly shut away from transmission

you are, in other words, everyone, except for
your little exception box to which you may

repair for repair or prayer when the wide
scene loses hold on its outlines: the more to

be said the closer you get to nothing: you
peep out at dawn and say of the whole thing,

look at that, when, later, looking at the
vibration in the microinscriptive, you may

need to call up libraries of language for
poise: it could not be truly said of the

yellowjackets that they are out in the drizzle
today without their jackets, even though it is

true that they are not without their jackets:
if god is in each of us, I wonder if he is

in each of the gorillas, if only in his
gorilla-aspect, a facet the gorillas can see

themselves and be seen by, just as, I suppose,
when we look, we see our own natures, native

and, like ligatures, sewn together: the
yellowjackets that usually streak straight into

the stone socket of the stone wall they nest
in, today buzz broadly about that wet entrance

before diving in: the yellowjacket god is these
motions, and when naked yellowjackets

dip and streak and hunt the clover blooms,
don't think they don't feel at home, right with

their god: for it is true far and wide that
nothing is so true as what breaks into being

this minute from colossal petrifications of
past time and huge issuances into time-to-be:

don't mess with me, or the yellowjackets: we
are in a high place which may or may not explode

but if it explodes nothing will be lost, every
little tiny atom will still be spinning for

the lord: we may go, and scientists may suck
the yellowjackets out of their hole to extract

the sting-venom: have no fear: weep but move
on: if the god is not in residence, he is in

motion, and it is hard to tell which is which:
coco rico, the rooster crows: it is day again.

Shit Face

What due's death's due: is death fifty/fifty
with life, or is there one thing only, life,

life merely ends: what difference, you say,
does it make: why, I suppose it makes a

difference: should you spend half your life
buddying-up with death or should you altogether

ignore it, since it is nothing, and think life,
life, life! and companion not at all with dark

consequence, a distant cousin: be not
reproachful if you find no scissors in me

cutting cleanly through this: I am too
concerned with whether I am one blade and

unable to gnaw or whether I command opposing
blades whose opposition draws a straight

slice: why, by the way, is direction in
opposition, while mere ineffectuality gapes

in singleness: single women who will not
chunk it up, why mere air will not slam it

down: I'm sure there's more to this than
meets the eye: with bursts of gamma rays

from unlocatable sources flashing around us,
I wonder how much of the universe's center

the new leaf on the philodendron can capture:
it is, after all, quite an emergence, timed

on December 19, just right for the lengthening
light, do you suppose: or did that watering

about a month ago, a long overdue soak, set
it off: I do not specialize in the causes of

anything, acceptance over explanation anytime
causes are the results of something else whose

results cause something else: still, I don't
think it just goes round and round, though it

goes round and round: I think there are some
little threads in there that feed in or peel

out, along with embroilment and hurling along
the central axis: but I don't believe for a

sec that a butterfly sinking down to suck salt from
a riverside causes a cyclone at sea: buildups

would be just fine if other buildups weren't
cutting them down, you bet your sweet bippy:

where is any action going to find a wide avenue
of gathering energy in: not the Champs thing:

not Park or Fifth: certainly, no winding
riverbed or former long lake dinosaurs got

washed away with when it cracked open ever so
many thousand years gone by: still, it is

largely true that eating too much fat fattens
people: anxiety, on the other hand, drains

you lean: fat and happy (or not so happy) or
scrawny and miserable (or quite light on your

feet): life, though, is terribly sad because
it apparently leads to death: unless, of

course, you need to get there, I hope you don't,
but you should hear the doctors laugh and

cringe at my medical theories about what
causes what: actually, I think, or they think

I think, or they just think that my theory
includes some psychology, like paranoia, say,

and hypochondria: well. . . .

Surprising Elements

The Ammons women (nine of them, my father's
sisters) were jovial women: well, I guess you

could say that: for them, the distance between
fun tears and tears was a flash of seconds:

Aunt Mitt used to say of some old scraggly man
that he was hopper-behind—hopper behinded?

she meant he was all shoulders (or belly) and
no backseat, just some draggy pants with nothing

back there to fill them out, a hopper, do you
reckon: I doubt she meant he was a hopper,

always looking to hop on something, if you get
my inclination: I think she meant something

to fill up, as in picking green beans in the
field and carrying them in a hopper: Aunt Mitt

died in the front bedroom: the parlor was on
the other side of this long hall: I stood in

line out on Aunt Mitt's porch when I was sixteen
to receive with others her coffin to put in the

hearse: I was a pallbearer: I was sixteen:
what I saw didn't sink in: I was thinking

something else: though I saw (and recall)
everything very clearly: the room she died in

exists nowhere now probably but in my head:
well, there may be one of her seven surviving:

it was a long time ago: I wish I knew: Aunt
Lottie was such an eager woman, so full of

life and laughter: what became of her will
make a short story long. . . .

Out From Under

Sometimes movies produce events to go with what
must be instead of letting what must be arise

from events: the first is contrived and
feebly illustrative, while the latter creates

the inevitability of what must come: all this
is known to everyone: I only look for another

set of words to say it: even if not well: a
try: can you imagine how wonderful it is not

to be on the track of a final draft but living
in an instantaneous veracity: but Johnson, I

think, said that easy writing makes hard
reading: oh, I wish I could have sat around

and belched a little with him, the immensity
of his philosophical centeredness occupied

with trivia and cold leg of lamb: even
if Moses had not clum up the mountain and

gotten scorched in the fire service, it would
be a good idea not to steal, lie, or mess with

your neighbor's wife: you could get killed or
hanged, where there's a distinction: you

really don't need a stone memento to sanction
what open dynamics clearly affirm: it is

better to honor your parents: you don't have
to agree with them: honoring is a peaceful

and informed transition: dishonor almost
certainly flares up unpleasantly privately

but also fractures the public order: so how
long do I have to go on about this. . . .

The Whole Situation

Don't stop or the past will catch up with you:
all the dumb things you said (for fun) will

overtake you and huddle around you pointing
serious fingers: redemption lies ahead if

only in a new relation to the past: for what
can redeem the past—a newer way of looking

at it in the future: for how can what is done
be undone: pay attention to something else:

forget about it: misremember it: ask for
forgiveness: do something else *good:* devise

distractions: keep busy: be up and about and
the ghostly leavings of events will lay down,

as with riverbeds, bottoms over bottoms, or
grow, as with coral seas, one thing on top of

another: up and about, you will find that
quick motions in the scenes and quick changes

of scene give a sense of fluidity to the hard
rock of fixation: take a pill: change the

mood and everything changes: thank the Lord
for change which often so much worsens the

world: the sun has had its earliest setting,
and Christmas is only a dusting white: I

remember an ancient Christmas morning with my
tin toy mule and milk wagon on the quilt:

I was four and that little thing tied a world
together: it was a miracle: but that is a

story too old to save. . . .

WE FORD LOW WATER AND FERRY DEEP

Rattling Freight Lines

December 30th and already the sun setting
cleared the crabapple tree branch northbound:

the sun, though, still rises later till, say,
the middle of January, but then day will widen

on both sides, opening like a flower, the mother
of all flowers: what summary learning is one

to take from all this: why, that it is some
of the world's oldest baggage, incredibly new:

we got our kicks in year 96 but will the market
be heaven in ninety-seven: oops, there it

goes, poetry again: rilly quaint: (actually,
I stand on the corner of the living room rug,

and *that* is what makes the sun always set
earliest behind the crabapple branch): (if

the rug slips or the branch sways, the whole
cosmos will be off:) (imagine an inch shifting

a nebula): it seems better not to make living
the object: because if living is the object,

death dismisses the proceeds: I presume I am
trying to make something, not a living surely:

what I am trying to make (prosetry?) prevents
me from undertaking the routes to living:

what would it mean to go in for living, what
would one do, apart, of course, from the

terror of the adamant scythe: abandon oneself
to one's appetites (eat, drink, be merry, for)

(the hornet's nest's paper weight gives spring
to the limb, a breeze that shivers empty twigs)

and complications right away arise. . . .

That's What I Just Got Through Saying

Shakespeare makes speaking, poetry: how does
he do that, anyhow: but, of course, nobody

in England ever talked liked that: or anywhere
else: but S distinguished between poetry and

prose, poetry metrical (and sometimes rimed):
so poetry, am I to think, is at least mechanically

metrical: but on the chance that tidal rhythm
which is the kind I write—prosetry—can be

allowed, I make a new word for it, probably
not new: prosetry, though, is a word for the

groundlings who are probably incapable of a
perception not a definition: I expect the

sensitive and listening to hear the music in
prosetry and be able to pick out the poetry

and then see that it prevails overall: or
else what is intelligence for: all that is

music from the past must be kept and all that
is sound given up: and new sound must ever so

subtly inform the old music (the deep silent
dynamics) and hold us safely in the arms of

our fathers, as we hold our children in our
arms: please, let's not hear anything more

about prosetry. . . .

It Doesn't Hold Water

So many people, you know, use their mouths as
an amusement park: they do rides on the

crunchymunchies, or slip down the slurp sluice,
or take in the carbonated baths, bubble burns,

or merry-go-round the chocolate box: this kind
of amusement, though, is like any other: you

have to pay for it: pounds and pounds and
pounds, and even some dollars: this amusement

feels light—indeed, *is*—but turns heavy:
still, I think you're better off using your

mouth for an amusement park than a playground:
whatever that is: careful with that one: my

advice is, use your mouth for a monastery and
keep the gate shut: or use it for a nunnery:

pray, and burn your fat and the candle's: I
find it awkward to type and eat (it is not

impossible to do so) so I type a lot: I melt
calories into letters: I have a letter box

like an ancient printer: his lead is my lead:
I hand type as he hand set: as I see him,

covered with ink and metal, I see him too busy
to eat: a ligature, a quarto, a folio, these

were his intervals, his lunch breaks: I see
him musing appreciatively over his work, a

lean person with a sober expression: he leans
back against the counter and doesn't get all

the lead off his fingers: (I think he has a
leather apron on): use your mouth as a

hangar and hold the words in or let them fly

Tom Fool

But what giving is to be expected from someone
who has nothing to give: and if one is to

have something to give, where is he to get it:
will others give it to him: let's say, not

consistently: and for what is given him, is
he to be paralyzed in a humiliation of

gratitude: can't one who has much give much,
if he will: where is one to acquire much,

except by making, keeping, and accruing, even
at a profit from others for services rendered:

if you have something to give, should you give
it to an individual who may be a wastrel or

vagabond, or should you give it to the
community as capitalization for business

activities bringing, maybe, jobs for carpenters,
word processors, software designers, so that

you make money yourself by giving, in a
sense, to all: well, you can see it isn't

easy, is it: look after yourself, you may be,
if inadvertently, looking after others: at

least, you won't be one yourself who needs to
be looked after by others: he creates a boon

who removes himself from welfare: as for me,
I am as much an innocent standbyer as bystander

which is to say, I may be participating even
when I am saying nothing, whenever that was:

but, all in all, the world doesn't make much
sense unless we make a little something up

TO GO WITH IT

Ringadingding

Dress up a charlatan like a lord, and who is
the lord: or don beggar's rags upon a beggar

and watch the curtseys stumble: if clothes
are the man, it is only so in consideration of

clothes—but since that consideration can
pass for the whole, man and all, it can be all:

the rich dress down and the poor up to achieve
true levels of participation that are truly

lies: well, misstatements of sign: you can,
indeed, not know the true man at all, if the

true man differs from the clothes he wears,
by the clothes he wears: I would have you

stumble there, as before the good writer
poorly dressed: looking good or bad, I pledge

to prefer no charge against myself: when the
police show up, I'll hire the best lawyer in

town and get off, tried or mistried: I'll pump
money into my lawyer, and his mouth will fly

with devices, exceptions, exemptions, and sweet
big words: I am not going to let myself lie

around undefended and defenseless: I haven't
done anything: I've done hardly anything now

for years: the sweetest leisure is work of
one's own choosing: (life is short, even when

it isn't): I mean, I haven't done anything the
law doesn't allow or can't find: but inside,

where the differences are, everybody is in
court, tongues and heads are flying and chains

are rattling: can, I cry out, we bring some of
these issues to trial: oh, no, when one is

oneself jury, accuser, pleader, judge subduing
the maelstrom lacks separation, the fiddling

aside of the plainly innocent: live for others:
living for others is life for oneself: live

for yourself, you put your self at odds with
all mankind, and you grow sour in your losses

or gains: cut off, you win or lose against
yourself, which is never winning: live for

others, not that they may live for themselves,
but that they, too, may live for others: life

for all can come of this, since giving is the
sweetest given, given back: the world's twisty

and the straightaway is crooked and the crooked
straightaway. . . .

I Wouldn't Go So Far As to Say That

The trouble with style is that it cannot look
ragged if clean cut, nor empty if full, nor

colorless if bejeweled: I mean, you would
think that: but so much colorful stuff is

trashy and boring, and serene emptiness is the
highest plane in some spheres, and raggedness

can look like clean displays of ruffles: I am
so impressed with the malleability of things

that I'm ready to let almost anything go: how
do you want the world, well, within reason,

have it any way you please: many can be boring
in their richest effort, but how can I be

plainly, truthfully boring except by being
boring (clever line break): and how can I

burst out into something if I already know the
program: but how can *you bear* exposure—and

why should you—to so much trot: I don't
know any reason except to be there when the

deal goes down, when competence stumbles and
reveals its dirty underclothes, or when the

spirit's whirlwind strikes the windy hills to
raise the dust: but I also wonder how you can

bear to be in the presence of the well-written
all the time: so, some little creep can iron

it out and measure it off, doodle some outlines
and make it look neat: let him: her: what to

do about style is one of my meanest problems:
I wrote some poems really short: I revised a

few till they were just perfectly revised: I
confess now to some interest in good bad

writing: I would just as soon see what I can
do about getting across the river when the

bridge floods out: what do I know: it may not
even rain: or if it rains, the sky may clear

so gloriously gold-fringed that I will weep:
prepared weeping may not achieve its tears,

but tears cannot be prevented when they have
to gather: this is an example: it's not

revised, it's bad, it's wonderful. . . .

Thrown for a Loop

There's so much more belief than truth, and
that is lucky in a way, belief inclining us

more toward what we need than what we'll get:
but we really do believe what we believe and

we hope it will work out: but put a plug of
gold on the scale opposite a sack full of

painted feathers, truth will that great woven
cluster outweigh: the fulcrum could be called

"getting along"—and that's where balanced
persons no doubt stand: those who slip down

the arm toward feathers keep an eye back on
truth, I'll bet, and those heavy with truth,

which is sometimes ruthlessly truth, oh, they
longingly look toward the painted fare: belief

can fulfill dramas of yearning, while truth's
exactions narrow down the margins: but even

when it's a tightrope it's somewhere to walk,
while dramas address theatrical appetites:

that truth and belief are one, cooperating one
with the other, that is simply GRAND, and they

sometimes do, aiming at heaven, cooperate: I
think that this means only that illusion plays

well against reality, though we have so much
trouble telling which is which, truth often

losing the figurements of its setup, and
illusion as often floating off, a grain of

reality its core: there is a sufficient place
in the mind that turns away into the errors

of explanation just to be about: the sitting
center's butt gets tired, and the feet and

legs can do with a little circulation, like
walking out into the country to chat with the

farmers, lend a hand, or help a calf stand up
in its freshest morning: do with the obvious:

little lies behind it. . . .

Wrong Road

So I said to the short-order cook (because I
think he owns the joint) what did Santa bring

you: a fairly aggressive bit of humor, since
I hardly know the man: my wife and I stop

there occasionally on the way to Syracuse
because it is so busy, the eggs are right, and

the waitresses friendly: when he says, Oh,
some of this and that: so I said, a boat:

(checking to see if he was really rich): a
gun, I said—maybe he was just one of the

guys: I have a lot of guns, he said: well,
I don't think he ever did say what he got,

some clothes, maybe: he was turning too many
eggs, jigging hash browns: on the way to

Syracuse, I finished it in my head: he got
angry: who's asking, he says: so I try to

bring him down: I'm too old to rise up to
risibility: I said, I'm a little older than

you, so I was wondering, because I was disappointed
in myself when my wife asked me before Xmas

what I wanted for Christmas: I couldn't think
of anything: what does it mean to want nothing

from Santa: so I just wondered what sort of
thing you might have wanted, or if you had

liked what you got: well (reader) this last
part doesn't sound as good as the way it came

to me around Lafayette: I have a little tingle
of fear that the next time I stop there, the

guy will say, listen, buddy, I'm old enough
you don't have to ask me what Santa brought me

and I'll say, well, it's Easter now, and I'm
not going to ask about *those* eggs. . . .

Way Down Upon the Woodsy Roads

Don't you think poetry should be succinct:
not now: I think it should be discinct: it

should wander off and lose its way back and
then bump into a sign and have to walk home:

who gives a hoot about these big-Mack trucks
of COMPRESSION: what are the most words for

the least: take your cute little compact and
don't tell me anything about it: just turn me

loose, let me rattle my ole prattle: poetry
springs greatest from deepest depths: well,

let her whistle: how shallow can anything
get: (rhyming on the front end): I do not

believe that setting words to rhyme and meter
turns prose into poetry, and having written

some of the shortest poems, I now like to
write around largely into any precinct (not

succinct) or pavilion (a favorite word) I fall
in with: I have done my duty: I am a happy

man: I am at large: life sho is show biz:
make room for the great presence of nothing:

do you never long to wander off: from the
concentrations: for it is one thing to fail

of them and another never to have intended
them: the love nest, men, becomes a solid

little (mortgaged) colonial: duty becomes your
chief commendation: the animal in you, older

than your kind, longs to undertake the heavy
freedom of going off by himself into the wide

periphery of chance and surprise, pleasure or
terror: oh, come with me, or go off like me,

if only in the deep travels of your soul, and
let your howl hold itself in through all the

forests of the night: it's the shortest day:
the sun is just now setting behind the branch

of the crabapple tree it always sets behind
this day of the year. . . .

DRAB POT